SRA
Reading Mastery
Signature Edition

Language Arts Textbook

Siegfried Engelmann
Karen Lou Seitz Davis
Jerry Silbert

Columbus, OH

SRAonline.com

 SRA

Send all inquiries to this address:
SRA/McGraw-Hill
4400 Easton Commons
Columbus, OH 43219

ISBN: 978-0-07-612566-1
MHID: 0-07-612566-1

3 4 5 6 7 8 9 10 QWV 13 12 11 10 09 08

D

	1. A big bird flew over our house.
	2. The car made a loud noise.

E

Rule: Sentences that report tell what the picture shows.

- Write **reports** if a sentence reports on what the picture shows.
- Write **no** if the sentence does not report.

1. Tom sat in a wheelchair.
2. Tom's sister walked next to him.
3. A nurse pushed a wheelchair.
4. The nurse felt very warm.
5. Tom was hungry.
6. Tom wore slippers and a hat.

- Write **reports** if a sentence reports on what the picture shows.
- Write **no** if the sentence does not report.

---

1. The woman rode a horse.
2. The horse was named Rusty.
3. The woman wore a hat and sunglasses.
4. The woman lived on a farm.
5. A man sat on the fence.
6. The man held a rope.
7. The man wanted to ride the horse.

E

A tall woman
Bill
The dog

Write sentences that report on the picture.

1.	________ held an umbrella.
2.	________ chased a cat.
3.	________ fell on the sidewalk.

D

1. Tom and his dog ran next to the lake.
2. They jumped in the water.
3. A little girl had a toy boat.
4. Sally and Ginger were under a tree.
5. They were happy.

Write sentences that report on the picture.

1.		sat in a wheelchair.
2.		pushed the wheelchair.
3.		stood next to the man.

For each picture, copy the sentence that tells the main thing the person did.

Mary held a glass.
Mary drank a glass of water.
Mary wore a belt.

Jill bent her leg.
Jill held the board with one hand.
Jill sawed a board.

- Write **reports** if the sentence reports on what the picture shows.
- Write **no** if the sentence does not report.

1. Mr. Jones stood in front of his desk.
2. Mr. Jones wore a shirt and tie.
3. Ned wrote on the chalkboard.
4. Ned was a very good speller.
5. One girl raised her hand.
6. Hilary held a piece of paper.
7. The room had desks in it.
8. Hilary raised her hand.

For each picture, copy the sentence that tells the main thing the person did.

1. Steve

Steve stood next to the tub.
Steve gave the dog a bath.
Steve held a brush in one hand.

2. Martha

Martha wore overalls.
Martha reached over her head.
Martha painted part of the house.

- Write **reports** if the sentence reports on what the picture shows.
- Write **no** if the sentence does not report.

1. Bill and Carlos sat in chairs.
2. Nancy read a book about horses.
3. The dogs dreamed about a bone.
4. Boots were on the floor.
5. All the fire fighters played cards.
6. Everybody wanted to go home.
7. Two dogs were lying on the floor.

Write the words that tell what people did.

1. give   2. dig   3. find   4. have   5. buy

 For each picture, copy the sentence that tells the main thing the person did.

1. Angela

Angela sat in a boat.
Angela loved the water.
Angela rowed a boat.

2. A boy

A boy held a broom.
A boy swept the floor.
A boy wore long pants.

3. Pam

Pam shoveled snow.
Pam stood in the snow.
Pam had a shovel.

Sentences that report on the main thing a person did have two parts. The first part of the sentence names the person. The second part tells the main thing the person did.

Write a sentence that reports on the main thing each person did.

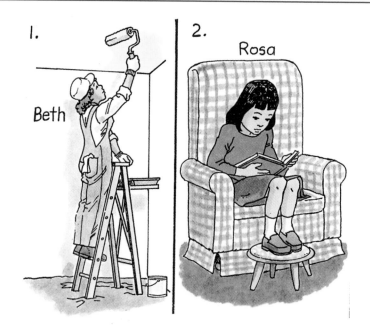

1.

Beth

2.

Rosa

| painted | book | ceiling | read |

Check 1

Does each sentence begin with a capital and end with a period?

Check 2

Does each sentence tell the main thing the person did?

Check 3

Did you spell words from the vocabulary box correctly?

A

> Write a sentence that reports on the main thing each person did.

1. A zookeeper

2. Bob

3. A girl

banana	pizza	cheese	campfire
log	built	gave	put	made

Check 1
Does each sentence begin with a capital and end with a period?

Check 2
Does each sentence tell the main thing the person did?

Check 3
Did you spell words from the vocabulary box correctly?

Read each sentence. Write the letter of each picture that shows what the sentence says.

1. A person held a hammer.
2. Seth held a tool.
3. Seth held a hammer.
4. A person held a tool.

Write a sentence that reports on the main thing each person did.

watering can   watered   ax

plant   tree   hanging   chopped

Check 1
Does each sentence begin with a capital and end with a period?

Check 2
Does each sentence tell the main thing the person did?

Check 3
Did you spell words from the vocabulary box correctly?

Read each sentence. Write the letter of each picture that shows what the sentence says.

1. Mark held a container.
2. Ashley held a jar.
3. A person held a container.
4. Ashley held a container.

Write a sentence for each picture. Each sentence should report on the main thing the picture shows.

1. Fred and Bill

2. A small dog

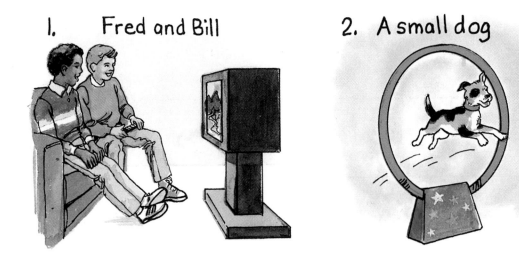

3. A young woman

| hoop | through | television |

Check 1
Does each sentence begin with a capital and end with a period?

Check 2
Does each sentence tell the main thing the persons or animal did?

Check 3
Did you spell words from the vocabulary box correctly?

D

Write the words that tell what people did.

1. see   2. go   3. sit   4. wear   5. run

E

Read each sentence. Write the letter of each picture that shows what the sentence says.

1. Brett ate fruit.

2. A person ate fruit.

3. Sandra ate an apple.

4. A person ate a banana.

Write a sentence for each picture. Each sentence should report on the main thing the picture shows.

1. Ramon

2. Yoshi

3. Jerry   Ann

poured	roasted	put	carried
soup	fire	marshmallows	

Check 1

Does each sentence begin with a capital and end with a period?

Check 2

Does each sentence tell the main thing the persons did?

Check 3

Did you spell words from the vocabulary box correctly?

D

Write the words that tell what people did.

1. sit   2. wear   3. run   4. see   5. go

E

Read each sentence. Write the letter of each picture that shows what the sentence says.

A.

B.

C.

D.

1. An animal wore clothing.
2. An animal wore a dress.
3. A dog wore clothing.
4. A cat wore a hat.

Write a sentence for each picture. Each sentence should report on the main thing the picture shows.

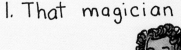

1. That magician

2. Hiro and his sister

3. The new carpenter

| jumped | carried | pulled | fence |
| boards | rabbit | over | |

Check 1
Does each sentence begin with a capital and end with a period?

Check 2
Does each sentence tell the main thing the persons did?

Check 3
Did you spell words from the vocabulary box correctly?

D Write the name for each group.

vehicles   children   fire fighters   men   horses

E Write a sentence for each picture. Each sentence should report on the main thing the picture shows.

1. A dog and a clown

2. The airplane

| flew | walked | tightrope | bridge | across | under |

Check 1

Does each sentence begin with a capital and end with a period?

Check 2

Does each sentence tell the main thing the person or thing did?

Check 3

Did you spell words from the vocabulary box correctly?

40000000131854

F Copy the paragraph.

 A bird fell out of a tree. It
landed on the ground. A boy picked
up the bird. He took it home.

Check 1

Does each sentence begin with a capital and end with a period?

Check 2

Did you indent the first line?

Check 3

Did you start all the other lines at the margin?

Rule: A paragraph is a group of sentences that tell about the same topic. You indent the first line of a paragraph. You start all the other lines right after the margin.

Copy the paragraph.

Ellen helped her dad fix the car. She worked on the brakes. Ellen and her dad fixed the car in three hours.

Check 1
Does each sentence begin with a capital and end with a period?

Check 2
Did you indent the first line?

Check 3
Did you start all the other lines at the margin?

E

Write the name for each group.

1.

2.

3.

4.

5.

6.

boys   girls   cars   women   police officers   dogs

Write a sentence for each picture. Each sentence should report on the main thing the picture shows.

1. The boy

2. A girl

| teeth | brushed | kicked | toothbrush | football |

Check 1
Does each sentence begin with a capital and end with a period?

Check 2
Does each sentence tell the main thing the person did?

Check 3
Did you spell words from the vocabulary box correctly?

D   Copy the paragraph.

> *Jason had a bad day. He*
> *missed breakfast because he woke*
> *up late. He had to walk to school*
> *in the rain.*

Check 1

Does each sentence begin with a capital and end with a period?

Check 2

Did you indent the first line?

Check 3

Did you start all the other lines at the margin?

 E   Read each sentence. Write the letter of each picture that shows what the sentence says.

1. He held a tool.
2. She held a hammer.
3. A person held a tool.
4. She held a tool.

F Write a sentence for each picture. Each sentence should report on the main thing the person did.

branch   water   sawed

Check 1

Does each sentence begin with a capital and end with a period?

Check 2

Does each sentence tell the main thing the person did?

Check 3

Did you spell words from the vocabulary box correctly?

D Copy the paragraph.

> *An eagle sat in a tree. It looked up into the sky. A big jet flew by. The eagle started to cry.*

E
- Write a sentence for each picture.
- Each sentence should report on the main thing the animal did.

1. A bear   2. A monkey

| walked | juggled | three | tightrope | across |

Check 1

Does each sentence begin with a capital and end with a period?

Check 2

Does each sentence tell the main thing the animal did?

Check 3

Did you spell words from the vocabulary box correctly?

Write a paragraph.

- Copy the sentence that tells the main thing the group did.

- Then write three more sentences. Write one sentence about each person. Tell the main thing each person did.

| hammer | side | board | nail | saw | paint |

	The women worked on the house.

Check 1

Does each sentence begin with a capital and end with a period?

Check 2

Does each sentence tell the main thing the person did?

A

Write a paragraph.

- Copy the sentence that tells the main thing the group did.
- Then write three more sentences. Write one sentence about each person. Tell the main thing each person did.

| washed | floor | picked | swept | dirt |
| toys | rug | pile | scrubbed | under |

The men cleaned the room.

Check 1

Does each sentence begin with a capital and end with a period?

Check 2

Does each sentence tell the main thing the person did?

Write a good sentence for each group.

| cleaned | elephant | basketball | washed |

Check 1
Does each sentence begin with a capital and end with a period?

Check 2
Does each sentence tell the main thing the group did?

Write a paragraph.

- Copy the sentence that tells the main thing the group did.
- Then write three more sentences. Write one sentence about each person. Tell the main thing each person did.

fried   poured   potato   soup

pieces   hamburgers   pot   sliced   fire

	Three cowboys made dinner.

Check 1

Does each sentence begin with a capital and end with a period?

Check 2

Does each sentence tell the main thing the person did?

A good sentence does two things. First, it names the group. Then it tells the main thing the group did.

| stream | room | cleaned | crossed |

Check 1
Does each sentence begin with a capital and end with a period?

Check 2
Does each sentence tell the main thing the group did?

F Write a paragraph.

- Copy the sentence that tells the main thing the group did.

- Then write three more sentences. Write one sentence about each animal. Tell the main thing each animal did.

A bear

A seal

A poodle

| bicycle | balanced | through | nose | its | ball |

	Circus animals did tricks.

Check 1

Does each sentence begin with a capital and end with a period?

Check 2

Does each sentence you made up report on the main thing the animal did?

D Write a good sentence for each group.

1.

2.

| opened | presents | water | pool | their |

Check 1

Does each sentence begin with a capital and end with a period?

Check 2

Does each sentence tell the main thing the group did?

Write a paragraph that reports on the picture.

- Begin with a good sentence about the janitors.
- Then write one sentence about each person.

chalkboard   desk   chair   cleaned   classroom   janitors

1. Copy the sentence that tells about all the pictures.
2. Copy the sentence that tells about only one picture.
3. Copy the sentence that tells about two pictures.

- He pushed a vehicle.
- She pushed a vehicle.
- A person pushed a vehicle.

> 1. Copy the sentence that tells about two pictures.
> 2. Copy the sentence that tells about all the pictures.
> 3. Copy the sentence that tells about only one picture.

Tom   Melissa   Melissa

- A person sat on an animal.
- He sat on an animal.
- Melissa sat on an animal.

E

Write a paragraph that reports on the picture.
- Begin with a good sentence about the gardeners.
- Then write one sentence about each person.

Raymond   Sally   Jill

gardeners	yard	carried	saw	plant
shovel	work	branch	hole	

F Write a good sentence for each group.

ate   through   snow   meal

Check 1
Does each sentence begin with
a capital and end with a period?

Check 2
Does each sentence tell the
main thing the group did?

Rule: Sentences have two parts—the subject and the predicate. The **subject** is the part of the sentence that names. The **predicate** is the part of the sentence that tells more.

Make up sentences by combining these subjects and predicates.

Subjects	Predicates
two old men	went to the store
my mother	worked in the yard
they	had a good time

 Write a paragraph that reports on the picture.
- Begin with a good sentence about the group.
- Then write one sentence about each person.

slide   yard   stood

1. Copy the sentence that tells about only one picture.
2. Copy the sentence that tells about all the pictures.
3. Copy the sentence that tells about two pictures.

- An animal sat on a bike.
- A dog sat on a vehicle.
- An animal sat on a vehicle.

Write a paragraph that reports on the picture.

- Begin with a good sentence about the group.
- Then write one sentence about each person.

| presents | string | opened | scissors |
| wrapping paper | | teddy bear | |

Check 1

Does each sentence begin with a capital and end with a period?

Check 2

Does each sentence tell the main thing the group did?

Check 3

Do the other sentences report on the main thing each person did?

E Make up sentences by combining these subjects and predicates.

Subjects	Predicates
everybody	drove to town
our teacher	got sunburned
she	paddled a canoe

F Write two sentences that report on the person.
- The first sentence should tell the main thing the person did.
- The second should tell something else about the person.

Mr. Harmon

radio   wore   mopped   listened   floor   kitchen   boots

Write two sentences that report on each person.

- The first sentence should tell the main thing the person did.
- The second should tell something else about the person.

1. A girl

2. Arthur

| baseball | caught | stood | glove | muscles |
| chopped | ax | uniform | fence |

E

1. Copy the sentence that tells about two pictures.
2. Copy the sentence that tells about all the pictures.
3. Copy the sentence that tells about only one picture.

- He pushed a truck.
- A person pushed a vehicle.
- A person pushed a car.

F

Write a paragraph that reports on the picture.

- Begin with a good sentence about the group.
- Then write one sentence about each person.

| cleaned | water | brush | scrubbed | washed |
| towel | dried off | poured | their | women |

Write a paragraph that reports on the picture.

- Begin with a good sentence that tells what the painters did.
- Then write two sentences about each person.
  The first sentence should tell the main thing the person did.
  The second sentence should tell something else about the person.

room	ceiling	painted	bottom	roller
kneeled	knees	brushed	ladder	used

Check 1

Does each sentence begin with a capital and end with a period?

Check 2

Did you write two sentences about each person?

Check 3

Does the second sentence about each person begin with **he** or **she?**

Write a paragraph that reports on the picture.

- Begin with a good sentence that tells what the waiters did.
- Then write two sentences about each person.
  The first sentence should tell the main thing the person did.
  The second sentence should tell something else about the person.

James   Joe

silverware   plates   table   placed

put   waiters   stack   set   held

Check 1

Does each sentence begin with a capital and end with a period?

Check 2

Did you write two sentences about each person?

Check 3

Does the second sentence about each person begin with **he?**

Write a paragraph that reports on the picture.

• Begin with a good sentence that tells what the girls did.

• Then write two sentences about each person.

stood	surfboard	swimming	pool	played
cap	wore	girls	water	jumped	nose

Check 1
Does each sentence begin with a capital and end with a period?

Check 2
Did you write two sentences about each person?

Check 3
Does the second sentence about each person begin with **she?**

| snake | striped | large | wooden | cowgirl |
| wearing | boots | outfit | young | basket |

Check 1

Does each sentence begin with a capital and end with a period?

Check 2

Does each sentence give a clear picture of what happened?

Subjects	Predicates
Mrs. Jones	ate breakfast
Fran and Jill	had new shoes
My uncle	ran every morning

beard   sailor suits   parrot   his shoulder   three   bald

Check 1

Does each sentence begin with a capital and end with a period?

Check 2

Does each sentence give a clear picture of what happened?

| skunks | muscles | tattoo | pie | piece |

Check 1
Does each sentence begin with a capital and end with a period?

Check 2
Does each sentence give a clear picture of what happened?

G

1. Write a sentence that tells only about picture A. Start your sentence with **The window.**

A. 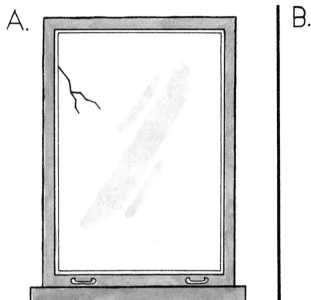   B.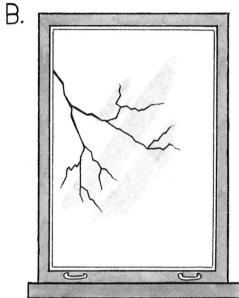

2. Write a sentence that tells only about picture A. Start your sentence with **The house.**

A.    B.

| woman | cactus | motorcycle | young |
| desert | wheel | mountain lion | |

Check 1

Does each sentence begin with a capital and end with a period?

Check 2

Does each sentence give a clear picture of what happened?

1. Write a sentence that tells only about picture A. Start your sentence with **A boy.**

A.

B.

2. Write a sentence that tells only about picture A. Start your sentence with **A painter.**

A.

B.

Pete   Jessica

Sally

Write a paragraph that reports on what happened.
Write a sentence for each name shown in the pictures.

1. A bluebird

2. A striped cat

3. The cat

4. The bird

5. The branch

6. The cat

ground	climbed	flew	jumped
landed	broke	trunk	branch

Check 1
Does each sentence begin with a capital and end with a period?

Check 2
Does each sentence tell the main thing?

Check 3
Does each sentence tell what somebody or something **did?**

Write the words that tell what somebody did.

1. draws   2. takes   3. comes   4. begins   5. swims

Write a paragraph that reports on what happened.
Write a sentence for each name shown in the pictures.

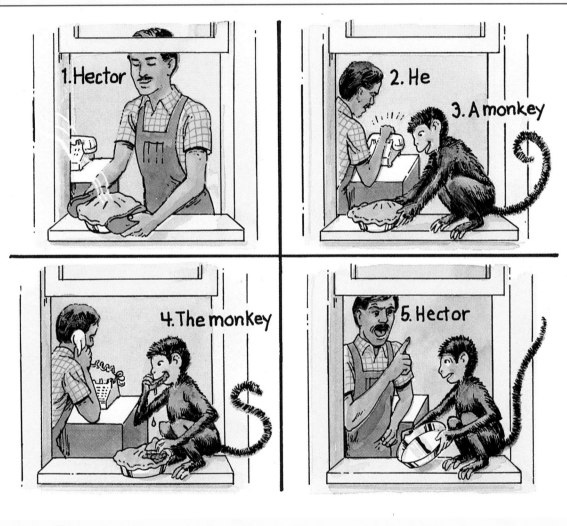

grabbed   window sill   started   yelled

ate   piece   pie   answered   phone   scolded

Check 1

Does each sentence begin with a capital and end with a period?

Check 2

Does each sentence tell the main thing?

Check 3

Does each sentence tell what somebody or something **did?**

D

1. Write a sentence that tells only about picture A.

2. Write a sentence that tells only about picture A.

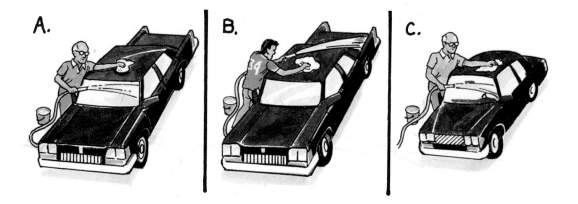

Write a paragraph that reports on what happened.
Write a sentence for each name shown in the pictures.

because   missed   head   threw   held   smelled   their

Check 1
Does each sentence
begin with a capital
and end with a
period?

Check 2
Does each sentence
tell the main thing?

Check 3
Does each sentence
tell what somebody
or something **did?**

Write a sentence that tells about only picture 1.

1.

2.

3.

Write a paragraph that reports on what happened.
Write a sentence for each name shown in the pictures.

carried   broke   pieces   brought   tripped   another

Check 1
Does each sentence begin with a capital and end with a period?

Check 2
Does each sentence tell the main thing?

Check 3
Does each sentence tell what somebody or something **did?**

Write a paragraph that reports on the picture.

- Begin with a good sentence that tells what the women did.
- Then write two sentences about each person.
  The first sentence should tell the main thing the person did.
  The second sentence should tell something else about the person.

| stream | canoe | backpack | crossed | carried |

Check 1

Does each sentence begin with a capital and end with a period?

Check 2

Did you write two sentences about each person?

Check 3

Does the second sentence about each person begin with **she?**

Write a paragraph that tells about the first picture, but not the second picture.

| scrubbed | roof | sponge | wheels |

Check 1

Does each sentence begin with a capital and end with a period?

Check 2

Does each sentence tell the main thing?

Check 3

Do the sentences give a clear picture of what the persons **did?**

1. Write two sentences about picture A.

- Begin your first sentence with **The dentist.** That sentence should tell what's **different** in picture A.

- Begin your second sentence with **He.** That sentence should tell the **main thing** the dentist did.

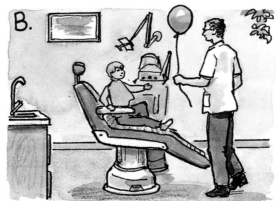

2. Write two sentences about picture A.

- Begin your first sentence with **The man.** That sentence should tell what's **different** in picture A.

- Begin your second sentence with **He.** That sentence should tell the **main thing** the man did.

E Write a paragraph that tells about the first picture, but not the second picture.

| high wire | juggled | wheel | bananas |

Check 1

Does each sentence begin with a capital and end with a period?

Check 2

Does each sentence tell the main thing?

Check 3

Do the sentences give a clear picture of what the clowns **did?**

D

1. Write two sentences about picture A.

• Begin your first sentence with **The woman.** That sentence should tell what's **different** in picture A.

• Begin your second sentence with **She.** That sentence should tell the **main thing** the woman did.

2. Write two sentences about picture A.

• Begin your first sentence with **The boy.** That sentence should tell what's **different** in picture A.

• Begin your second sentence with He. That sentence should tell the **main thing** the boy did.

E   Write a whole paragraph that tells about the first picture, but not the second picture.

| fire fighters | window | through | chopped | hose | climbed |

Check 1
Does each sentence begin with a capital and end with a period?

Check 2
Does each sentence tell the main thing?

Check 3
Do the sentences give a clear picture of what the fire fighters did?

1. Write two sentences about picture A.

- Begin your first sentence with **The girl.** That sentence should tell what's **different** in picture A.

- Begin your second sentence with **She.** That sentence should tell the **main thing** the girl did.

2. Write two sentences about picture A.

- Begin your first sentence with **The woman.** That sentence should tell what's **different** in picture A.

- Begin your second sentence with **She.** That sentence should tell the **main thing** the woman did.

1. Steve bent down and picked up a pencil.

2. Three girls watched a movie and ate popcorn.

3. He brushed his teeth and washed his face.

Write a whole paragraph that tells about the first picture, but not the second picture.

salad   sliced   meal   sprinkled   tomatoes   hamburgers

Check 1
Does each sentence begin with a capital and end with a period?

Check 2
Does each sentence tell the main thing?

Check 3
Do the sentences give a clear picture of what the cooks did?